For Erin, my coauthor

Farrar Straus Giroux Books for Young Readers
175 Fifth Avenue, New York 10010

Copyright © 2014 by Brandon Stanton
Color separations by Embassy Graphics Ltd.
Printed in China by South China Printing Co. Ltd.,
Dongguan City, Guangdong Province
Designed by Anne Diebel
First edition, 2014
1 3 5 7 9 10 8 6 4 2

mackids.com

Library of Congress Cataloging-in-Publication Data
Stanton, Brandon.
    Little Humans / Brandon Stanton. — First Edition.
        pages cm
    Audience: Age 4–8.
    ISBN 978-0-374-37456-3 (hardcover)
    1. Infants — Pictorial works — Juvenile literature.   2. Parent and child — Juvenile literature.   I. Title.
HQ781.5.S73 2014
305.232 — dc23
                                                                    2014010839

Farrar Straus Giroux Books for Young Readers may be purchased for business or promotional use.
For information on bulk purchases please contact Macmillan Corporate and Premium Sales Department at
(800) 221-7945 x5442 or by email at specialmarkets@macmillan.com.

BRANDON STANTON
LiTTLE HUMANS

FARRAR STRAUS GIROUX / NEW YORK

Little humans can do BIG things,

if they stand up tall

and hold on tight.

Sure, sometimes they fall.

But they get back up.

They'll be alright!

Little humans can be tough,

super tough,

super HERO tough!

But not too tough to need a hug,

or need some friends,

or need some love.

Little humans can put on a show,

to make you proud of what they know!

They help,

they play,

they slide in snow!

They spill,

they learn,

and then they grow!

Little humans can do such big things!

And say, "I did it myself!"

But if a thing's a bit too big,

they can say, "I need some help."

With all that little humans do,

like bend,

and twirl,

and dig,

don't be surprised if one says to you . . .

"Hey! I'm not little. I'm BIG!"